Still Propped Up at the Bar

Still Propped Up at the Bar

Katherine Baer

*This book is dedicated
to*

*my sisters
Janet and Chris*

*To have a loving relationship
with sisters
is not just to have two girlfriends
and confidantes
but to have two soul mates
for life*

Contents

The beauty of the world has two edges, one of laughter,
one of anguish, cutting the heart asunder.

Virginia Woolf

Foreword

For a woman without an alcohol problem, perhaps the title of this book seems a bit puzzling. Imbibing has proven to be my frequent friend and rarely my foe.

Early on (at the unsurprising age of 18, in the fall of my freshman year of college) I got a proper walloping from alcohol that has stayed with me a lifetime. An Airman stationed at Pease Air Force Base in New Hampshire, my boyfriend at the time, urged me to find a way to visit him. We conspired to arrange a weekend of sin, and I discovered again how adept he was at lying. At his request, a fellow Airman (one who apparently had a decent English teacher somewhere along the line) wrote a forged letter, supposedly from their commanding officer, promising my parents that I would be a guest at his home where I would be chaperoned by him and his wife for the weekend. My parents (bless them) were naive to the core and allowed me to purchase a train ticket, probably without a single thought that their good little daughter could be anything but good. A long distance phone call was a big deal at the time and a formal letter carried weight. Viola! The plot was set.

I rattled along train tracks for many long hours that Friday, stopping at every Podunk station along the way. Arriving tired but eager, I was greeted by a horny young man who had attempted too late to 'set the scene.' Yes, he'd nervously booked a motel room but hadn't thought of ice or food. My sole refreshment was a bottle of bourbon and a warm glass.

Guilt, nervousness, and an empty stomach aren't good drinking companions; I slugged down several drinks within a rather short period of time.

Details of embarrassing moments cling to you forever. In this case, it is the memory of yellow and orange shag carpet. (Shag carpeting was the new rage in decorating because of its soft and bouncy appearance. It was difficult to clean, though, and carpet rakes were often used to restore its looks.)

I began to vomit somewhere between ardent petting and pulling down the covers. When spewed upon a shag carpet, throw-up damage magnifies. I was beyond rectifying the situation in even a small way and could only stagger back and forth to the bathroom (which I also destroyed). The night that followed remains foggy to me but probably not to him. Perhaps he spent time between mopping up with all available towels and washcloths fabricating lies about fabulous sexcapades he'd tell to his buddies.

Although the night was a blur, the morning arrived with full, over-the-top, blasting sunshine that heightened my suffering. Even with bodily fluids long since depleted, my stomach refused to quiet and continued to lurch. We spent Saturday attempting to restore me enough for the ten-hour drive facing us on Sunday. The drive turned into an ordeal of misery, obliterating the splendor of a magnificent autumn day. For the first couple of hours, I'd beg him periodically to pull the car over to the side of the road 'just in case.' He washed and polished his car obsessively, so the thought of me soiling it must have been torture laid on top of torture.

Lucky for me I was returned to my dorm room and not my parents' home that Sunday evening. One look and they would have known that something awful had befallen me. As it was, my sympathetic floor mates greeted me with the appreciative stares of dumb adolescents who respect a colossal binge.

One other notable alcoholic memory bears repeating. But I'll save that for later . . .

I wrote *Who's the Old Broad at the Bar?* less than three years ago, but a lot has happened since. Let's just say some of it has been sobering. (Sorry. I'll be finished with the figurative use of alcohol shortly.) I'm a bit less sassy perhaps, but I continue to marvel at the richness of my life. So what is the bar upon which I prop myself?

Several times a week, that bar is an actual 'bring-out-the-bottle bar,' whether it's in the comfort of my condo kitchen, a restaurant, or some more exotic location. Wine and vodka soften my sharper edges when taken in moderation.

More importantly, though, the bar is a metaphysical support—an amalgam of life skills that allows me to muster on. Partly it's the stubbornness of aging. Partly it's curiosity. In large part it's certainly love. Allow me, please, to indulge in a few more ramblings . . .

Conveniently Seductive

There are no shortcuts to any place worth going.

Beverly Sills

Watching Birney burnish the newly cut edges of my ordinary door key, I saw the magic of his disciplined hands examining for the precision he required, his practiced eye deciding upon further exactitude. Applying the metal brush a bit more, he reached satisfaction. Each movement was self-assured and steady, the result of dedicated patience and practice. My attentive gaze mattered not; he would have performed identically alone.

I could have tried the new, shiny automated key-making kiosk. It had appeared since my last visit to Lowe's and reminded me of the coin-operated games that grab plush toys with a metal claw. I'd been conned out of quarters on those big teases, and sure enough, I soon discovered that the same CEO who created and owned those machines was the entrepreneur behind this new convenience. As of fall 2011, one hundred MinuteKey machines had been located in big-box stores in fifteen states, so the one I encountered was among the first.

It looked fail-safe glossy. Pick a design, insert your original key, insert your credit card, and voila!

Hesitating momentarily, I realized that despite the occasional inept hardware employee (whose duplicates failed to turn in the intended lock and caused me to gnash my teeth all the way back to the store), I actually enjoyed talking to a guy (so far no gals) while my keys were duplicated. And so I found Birney. He even slid the duplicate on my key ring, checking to make sure all the jagged edges of the multiple keys fell to the same side—a detail unimportant to many but necessary for perfectionists.

I could only imagine the snickers of certified locksmiths about these key-making kiosks. Like many tantalizing gadgets, they offer the illusion that technology can offer simplicity in our complicated lives. Sure, within a very narrow range, these machines may serve a purpose, but if I had enough venture capital to sit on the Shark Tank panel, I would have passed on this one. There's a Vending Machine Frustration Group on Facebook for a reason.

Speaking of illusory simplicity . . . I often labor under the illusion that with focused determination I can manage to make the important people in my life behave as I would choose for them to behave (despite an avalanche of evidence to the contrary). The primary minefield for this warped thinking is my six-year relationship with the man in my life.

In his best-selling book *DON'T SWEAT THE SMALL STUFF . . . and it's all small stuff,* Richard Carlson observed, "Whenever we are attached to having something a certain way, better than it already is, we are almost by definition, engaged in a losing battle. Rather than being content and grateful for what we have, we are focused on what's wrong with something and our need to fix it."

It's laughable that I've read that advice, re-read that advice, highlighted that advice, memorized that advice so many times and yet can't seem to own it. In my long-term relationships with men, I'm compelled to 'fix them' over and over and over again. It's somewhat incredible that I've never been the victim of a murder investigation.

I tend to do a great deal of mental snowballing. Sadly for the men I've loved and still love, they're usually not aware of the size of the accumulating snowball until it runs them over.

Most women seem to have a primal urge to clean closets at the beginning of a new year. It's a female metaphor for setting things right before moving on. I begin cleaning closets as soon as the first chill follows summer. It builds and builds with the coming holidays (in my family, one huge orgiastic continuum of Halloween-Thanksgiving-Christmas) and climaxes right before New Year's Day.

Matt recognizes the signs but is powerless to defend himself. The last holiday season, I managed to keep it in check until January 2. One more day and he would have escaped unscathed back to his home at the beach (alas, only a postponement of the inevitable).

In a book about the importance of metaphor in the craft of writing, American author Janet Burroway contends that symbols are unavoidable to convey meaning. She says, "We must [use symbols] because we rarely know exactly what we mean, and if we do we are not willing to express it, and if we are willing we are not able, and if we are able we are not heard, and if we are heard we are not understood. Words are unwieldy and unyielding, and we leap over them with intuition, body language, tone and symbol."

A New Year's Day football party provided an unlikely metaphor—a coffee maker—for what was brewing in me (pardon the pun).

My dislike for two of the most loved beverages, beer and coffee, often makes me feel like a misfit in some fundamental, hormonal way. One or both of them is a common denominator at virtually all gatherings and the shared imbibing is an assumption. Tea, which I love, is often overlooked or an afterthought, and wine (although popular) still can't hold a candle to beer when it comes to down-home, cheap refreshment. Two sacred Maryland past-times— watching football and eating crabs—necessitate an appreciation of the brew.

Anyway, at this particular football party, Matt and I were initiated into an apparently widespread practice that had formerly escaped our attention, the worship of K-cups. It seemed that we were the only attendees ignorant of this technological wonder. The mighty Keurig machine occupied a position of honor in the kitchen, accompanied by its own specially designed carousel filled with tantalizing varieties of coffee (mainly) and a smattering of tea, hot cocoa, and hot apple cider. Matt was led to the coffee altar and quickly succumbed to its charms. Because this Keurig model was 'top-of-the-line,' it provided a reservoir of water that could provide for multiple cups. Each thirsty individual selected his/her own particular beverage choice from the cute carousel of little cups resembling creamers in restaurants (but a bit larger), and popped it into the high-tech mechanism that rose as a gleaming handle was lifted. Blue and red brewing lights heightened the anticipation of a single perfect cup. Wow.

The next morning was Sunday morning, a ritualistic day for us as a couple, one begun with Matt's trip to the local 7-Eleven for copies of *USA Today*, *The Baltimore Sun*, *The Washington Post*, and *The New York Times*. These loaded Sunday editions have the collective weight of a five-pound bag of sugar. Placed as an offering at my feet, these last vestiges of print journalism represent something shared and solid about us as a couple. He acknowledges my need for a paging-turning, ink-rubbing wallow in these papers throughout the day (often culminating back in the same bed before midnight and lights out). We're of the same vintage within a year, so newspapers have always been a comforting regularity in our lives, although in recent years our daily subscriptions have fallen aside as they have for most people. Our e-reading news forays substitute for the paper on the doorstep six days a week, but on Sunday, we embrace 'hard copy' in the same way we return to classic rock radio semi-automatically at regular intervals.

I hasten to add that Sunday is not totally given over to newspaper reading, but it is the start-up we both love. Even if we are off and running to a tailgate or family gathering of some sort, the paper waits for its due time. Obsessive types will understand that I always save my favorite, *The New York Times*, for last.

On this particular Sunday, the first of 2012, a litany of concerns had implanted themselves in my brain. All of them centered on relationship issues. Like the unruly, unsorted socks in his underwear drawer, there was no order to my repetitive thoughts, but after rattling and nagging at me for weeks, they ached to come out. (Again, "We rarely know exactly what we mean . . .") I was nervous. Matt had been through several cycles of my mental house cleaning but perhaps this time it would come out all wrong and he'd resent it.

We began to revisit the Keurig conversation from the night before. Both of us intended to get one of the damn things in response to the rapture of our friends at the football party. What ensued was a painstakingly detailed discussion of size, function, cost, and usage. Seldom do couples engage in such an animated, lengthy conversation about a coffee maker as we did that morning. I urged it along in an attempt to suppress my inner demons. I think Matt was just curious in a practical sense. Finally the talking wore itself out.

"Maybe the Keurig is comparable to the way our relationship is working," I offered without forethought.

Matt's response was a thoughtful, knowing silence. Bless him, he gets me. I didn't have to spell it out. Finally I knew what was troubling me, and finally he knew not only that something was troubling me, but also what it was. The coffee maker had become a clear, understandable symbol for something complex.

Ahhhh . . . the imaginative transcendence of ordinary experience.

Had our 'Once Upon a Time Romance' faded? Had we become like the automatic, put-in-a-Kcup, get out a predictable output kind of couple? Had our A+ exciting, passionate relationship slipped to a B+ better-than-most, consistent relationship?

As a couple (but probably mostly me), we don't want to settle for lukewarm. We've felt the heat. Matt seems happier with contentment than I do. I must always push our relationship; Matt doesn't feel the need to.

It's no earth-shaking observation to say relationships are hard work, but most of us blunder through the hard work, sometimes producing disastrous results when what we really want to do is tune things up a bit.

Matt continues to astound me with the generosity of his spirit. Rather than resent my suggestions that he needed to work harder on a couple of things, he responded with warmth and affirmation.

I thrive on dynamic tension. I make myself feel guilty about this sometimes, but that's just the point. I make myself feel guilty, nobody else does, especially not Matt. He wouldn't love me as much if I became lower-keyed; he fell in love with a pushy (assertive), controlling (purposeful) woman, and he can live with that.

When you buy that expensive, shiny new coffee maker, you don't want to hear about banging on it for a full cup, or de-scaling it, or operating on it with a paper clip. When the first roses come and the first champagne is drunk, you never want to imagine cleaning your lover's toothpaste spit from the sink either.

After that Sunday morning conversation, I visited multiple blogs about Keurigs:

"We were having trouble getting the full amount of coffee so we ran vinigar [sic] through it and flushed it out real good. The nex day she when hay wire, the 6 once light didnt light up. Then they all died then they all went out. now i have a $120 dollar paper wieght."

"Finally my peaceful husband has slapped it, starring hopelessly into the eye of the kcup dispenser wondering what has gone wrong."

Yes, I bought a Keurig . . . and about a hundred dollars worth of assorted K-cups. (You can't help yourself once you've taken the plunge.) The thrill of the first cup (tea, not coffee) dissipated pretty quickly, but at least my coffee-drinking visitors will have proof of my sincere desire to please them. Judging from the evidence, it probably won't last nearly as long as a 1980's Mr. Coffee.

I'm not giving away those pesky coffee filters in the top of my pantry any time soon. I'm trying not to be too pessimistic after reading that FedEx deliverymen joke about the regularity of Keurig replacements they deliver to disappointed customers. I'd like this machine to deliver on its promise of quality *and* simplicity. But I doubt it. Like relationships, it's often the messiness of the process that makes for a great cup of coffee or a great love affair.

Allow me, please, indulgence in another favorite movie moment. I'm such a sucker for good dialogue. This one comes from the film *As Good As It Gets*.

Melvin (played by Jack Nicholson): I've got a really great compliment for you, and it's true.

Carol (played by Helen Hunt): I'm so afraid you're about to say something awful.

Melvin: You make me want to be a better man.

If I could yank those lines right out of that movie and steal them to insert in my life, I'd die from ecstasy.

Wait a minute! I _have_ lines from my life as good as that to fondle in my dotage. One of the great gifts I own is that I've been loved unconditionally.

It doesn't get better than that.

Painters creating Natty Boh billboard on building, 1974

"The only time a woman really succeeds
in changing a man is when he is a baby."

Natalie Wood

Bus Ride

We must remember the past, define the future, and challenge the present—whenever and however we can. It will take the rest of our lives even to begin.

But then, what else have we to do?

Jane O'Reilly

Time magazine said of 1968, "Like a knife blade, the year of riot and revolution severed the U.S. from its triumphant optimism, exposing a confused, divided country . . ."

On April 4th, the day Martin Luther King, Jr. was assassinated, I was almost twenty-three and pregnant with my second child. On the same day, a twenty-one-year-old seminarian at St. Gregory's in Cincinnati, Ohio decided to sneak off campus with a friend. The two of them stashed their cassocks under a tree, caught a bus into the city, and looked forward to visiting a new mall. ("A whole bunch of stores indoors, all under one huge roof . . . no way!")

The nation had barely absorbed LBJ's announcement that he would not seek re-election when, five days later, Martin Luther King, Jr. was hit in the neck by a rifle bullet on a balcony of the Lorraine Motel in a black neighborhood in Memphis.

Lured by the rumor that you could see Vanessa Redgrave's breasts in the movie *Camelot*, the two young students headed for the movie theater. There were no breasts to be seen, but the real adventure of the day was yet to be revealed. Curiously, they had probably mistaken the tantalizing prospect of exposed breasts with Redgrave's role in *Blow-Up* from two years earlier in 1966 when she portrayed a woman in the first British film to display full-frontal nudity, a film provocative and liberal, unlike the film *Camelot* in which Redgrave played Guinevere. Apparently, it didn't take much to stir the imagination of male seminarians headed for a life of celibacy.

After the movie, the two miscreants caught the bus headed back to St. Gregory's, probably thinking they would get away with their excursion as they had many times before. What were the odds they would pick the very day of an earth-shattering event for their mischief? As the bus moved into Avondale, a black section of Cincinnati, frenzied rioters bent on expressing their outrage halted them. The seminarians had no idea what had provoked the fury, but they found themselves in the center of a maelstrom. The bus was rocked and pelted. For a seemingly endless time, the prospect of danger loomed, and even the arrival of Cincinnati policemen couldn't turn the tide. Eventually, the National Guard arrived.

News of the rioting reached St. Gregory's via local television, and so, when the bus was eventually freed and made its way back to Mt. Washington, the young men emerged from the bus to face the Monsignor.

I'm a bit puzzled about why I can't recall what I was doing when the news broke about MLK. Even my friend in New Zealand remembers exactly where she was when she heard. The only explanation is that I had a toddler about to turn two in the same month, and, as I've already said, I was pregnant. Young motherhood is so all-consuming that events beyond the household fall on a fuzzy periphery unless they directly impact the safety or well being of the nest. Even so, it seems remarkable to me now that I have only a vague recollection of the Baltimore race riots that began two days after the assassination. During the ensuing days up until April 14, thousands of National Guard troops struggled to contain the frenzied anger and grief of people long denied full citizenship. Cruelly stripped of nonviolent leadership, their guts told them that the more radical voices long quelled by King's patience had been right about taking what you feel you need from America. Only twelve miles separated me from the fray, and yet, I don't remember being terrified. Frightened, yes, but in a buffered 'the suburbs are surely safe' kind of way.

I have no recollection of what I was doing the day Robert Kennedy was shot just three months after MLK. It seems impossible to me now that I was so buffered from the shocking blows of 1968. Only a month prior to delivering my daughter, RFK's death didn't shake me out of my Pollyanna 'rise and shine' optimism. My brother Carl, four years younger than I, chose never to have children because (as he said late in his teens) "I won't bring a child into this awful world." The events of Vietnam and the double assassinations cast a cynicism upon him that skipped me.

I remember the Democratic National Convention in Chicago that August more, probably because it was televised and I was spending a lot of time housebound that summer. Nursing a six-week old baby gives you your only opportunity to sit still after childbirth. I remember Nixon's selection of our Maryland governor, Spiro Agnew, as his running mate because it seemed like an honor for the state, but it was many years later before I realized that Agnew's tough stance with the Baltimore rioters drew Nixon's attention.

That unlucky seminarian, who experienced the fury of heart-broken blacks first hand in a bus taken captive, actually attended the Democratic National Convention rather than watching it from a couch. As our lives converged decades later and I listened to his stories, I realized how apolitical I'd been during my early twenties. My parents had been Republicans and Dwight Eisenhower had been the comforting president of my childhood. It's hypocritical of me to urge eighteen-year-olds to participate in elections. True, I've never failed to vote in an election, but my full, informed awareness of politics had to wait until my reproductive phase had run its course.

Actually, though, I couldn't vote when I was eighteen. It was illegal for me to buy an alcoholic beverage until after my first child was born. (Jeff was born on April 24, 1966 and my twenty-first birthday wasn't until May 16, 1966.) What seems odder is that I was not eligible to vote for President of the United States until after I was the mother of two. The voting age was twenty-one, and there was no presidential election in the year I turned twenty-one (1966). I had to wait until November 1968 to cast my first 'big vote.' I'd give $1000 to know with absolute certainty that I voted for Hubert Humphrey against Richard Nixon, but the truth is, I don't think I did. I was a Kennedy fan, true, but I don't think I thought of myself as a Democrat until Vietnam changed the landscape, and besides, there was the Agnew thing. I know absolutely that I voted for McGovern in 1972, but that was a negative vote against Nixon more than enthusiastic support for McGovern. Truthfully, I know almost nothing about George McGovern to this day.

Richard Nixon signed Amendment Twenty-six into law on July 5, 1971, granting the right to vote at age eighteen. At the signing in the East Room, Nixon talked about his confidence in the youth of America. That's pretty ironic, isn't it, given what we know about youthful distrust of Nixon in the re-election of 1972?

So after attending the 1968 Democratic National Convention, who do you think that young seminarian voted for in November 1968? Nixon? Wrong—although a good guess since his uncle, for whom he was named, was the pilot who flew Nixon around in Air Force Two when Nixon was Vice President under Eisenhower. Humphrey? Wrong. Nope, he voted for write-in candidate Dick Gregory, a black civil rights activist and comedian. His vote was one of 47,097 cast for Gregory, a man he'd met in southern Indiana prior to the election. After his impressive speech, Gregory shook the young man's hand and asked, "Will you vote for me?" "Yes," he answered. True to his word, he did. There was a chasm of some magnitude between the suburban Baltimore woman I was at the time and the urban Chicago man he was. But it makes for fascinating (endless) conversations between us now.

U.S. Congresswoman Pat Schroeder once said, "There is this idea that you can stay home and make the world better for your family—well, you can make it a whole lot better for a lot more people if you get out and do something about public policy." That observation makes me squirm. She served in the House of Representatives for twenty-four years and did so while the mother of two kids, just like me. When asked by a male colleague how she could be a woman and serve in Congress, she famously answered, "I have a brain and a uterus, and I use them both."

Many women like me had more power than we ever realized we had and didn't recognize it until much later. Even given the chance, I wouldn't have been happy as a politician like Pat Schroeder. (But boy, would I love to have dinner with her!) Looking back from this vantage point though, I would wish from myself more political involvement and bravery as time went along. I wish I could recount to my grandchildren stories about my march in a civil rights demonstration or an anti-Vietnam protest. Watchers are a dime a dozen.

In the winter I began to tutor two of my grandsons, Patrick and Collin. Because they are separated in age by only eighteen months, it's possible to strike a common instructional ground between them, and their fondness for one another makes time spent with them a joy.

Each tutoring session began with a segment I called 'Teach Me Something' during which they recalled something learned in school (Patrick in 6th grade, Collin in 5th) and taught it to me. This enabled me to share in their public school experiences and check their comprehension. In one session, Collin chose to teach me about MLK. Turns out, his music teacher witnessed the "I Have a Dream" speech in 1963. They'd just had a three-day weekend because of the MLK birthday commemoration that Monday, a floating holiday that occurs the third Monday in January. When South Carolina became the last state to accept an MLK state holiday in 2000, all fifty states finally adhered to the national holiday signed by Reagan in 1983. My grandsons are delightfully unaware of the controversy surrounding the holiday.

I've thought a lot about the naivety of my younger years. (Notice I didn't say 'innocence.' Dating a daring guy more than three years older when I was just fifteen took the edge off innocence.) But certainly I was naïve. Partly this was because, in my household, adult conversations were kept separate from us kids. Our 1950's *Leave It To Beaver* lifestyle didn't prompt much thought about politics, nor did it open me to the richness of diversity. It would probably have mattered if I had known even just a few people who weren't Caucasians.

I think a lot now about what I'd like my grandchildren to know. Certainly at the top of the list is an awareness of the difference between passing a class and really learning something. I hope they will maintain a healthy curiosity that will serve them well personally and in the world at large. If they can pay attention to life now in a way that really matters, they will be much more likely to end up happy.

Tutoring ain't what it used to be. Their iPad and mine stood ready to check facts; loaded with dictionaries, bookstores, and an abundance of utilities, they served a vital role as fourth players in our time spent at the wooden kitchen table. In between actual sitting together times, we stayed connected electronically.

"How many U.S. Presidents have been assassinated? Love you! Mama Baer" (my email to the boys the day after the tutoring session mentioned above)

"2" (answer sent back)

"Nope. That's not the correct answer."

"what but it's Abraham Lincoln and John F Kennedy"

"Google it and send back the right answer."

"it's 4"

"There you go!"

American educator Virginia Gildersleeve said, "The ability to think straight, some knowledge of the past, some vision of the future, some skill to do useful service, some urge to fit that service into the well-being of the community—these are the most vital things education must try to produce."

Dinner was a significant part of our tutoring. At the table, I prompted the kids to share what we'd studied during our session. The six of us (daughter Karen, son-in-law Kevin, Kelsey and the two boys, plus me) valued the chance to lock eyes over the food, delighting in the stimulation of focused conversation. I didn't side-step adult topics; we discussed NASA, the coming presidential election in November 2012, the Summer Olympics in London, and the significance of Pearl Harbor. Without fail, viewing events or history through young eyes refreshed my perceptions.

One of my ongoing goals is to enhance their command of words so that they move forward with a mastery of English that will give them an advantage in life. We eyeball words, experiment with them, alter them, employ them, and play with them. The word *barrier* was presented in the vocabulary book we used as a foundation. A question was asked about what barriers an early female physician had to overcome. The boys were stumped. Growing up in a household where their father encourages their sister and mother to attempt whatever they wish (and within an extended family in which females flourish in formerly male-dominated roles), it's inconceivable to them that women were once blocked from becoming doctors. Their eyes widened in response to my explanation; my heart sings at such moments.

It seems not at all strange to them that we have a black president. The painful journey from 1968 to 2008 was not and never will be their journey. Their childhood memories will include Barack Obama just as my childhood memories include Dwight Eisenhower. I've come to respect my role as grandparent more and more as my grandkids emerge as people from babyhood and toddlers. There's magic to those early years of being Mama Baer, for sure, that will always warm me, but I'm loving their emergence as distinct young people with potential and contributions in the making. A house needs grandparents in it, not daily, but in good measure. I can help them make sense of Sputnik; they will help me make sense of what is yet unimagined.

Many people keep calendars for a full year in advance, as I do, but I also keep a calendar that stretches farther into the future. The happiest dates on my calendar are graduations in 2014 (Kelsey), 2018 (Patrick), 2019 (Collin), 2022 (Cooper), and 2027 (Nate). I intend to be there for every one of them.

American educator Edith Hamilton said, "It has always seemed strange to me that in our endless discussions about education so little stress is laid on the pleasure of becoming an educated person, the enormous interest it adds to life. To be able to be caught up into the world of thought—that is to be educated."

My most treasured hope for my grandchildren (in addition to finding love, of course) is that they will find delight and fulfillment in education. I will plant as many seeds as I can and then celebrate the wonderfulness within them that unfolds.

Family observes woman with dog,
near Ellicott City, 1973

"Those who can serve best, those who help most, those who sacrifice
most, those are the people who will be loved in life and honored in
death, when all questions of color are swept away and when in a free
country free citizens shall meet on equal grounds."

Annie Besant, English writer (1847-1933)

The Demon in the Closet

Happiness is the light on the surface of the water.
The water is dark and deep.

T he darkest thing in our lives became first apparent during one of the happiest of moments for our family. In May 1990, my oldest niece was to be married, and the occasion was even more anticipated because our kid brother Dave—the youngest of five—was to arrive from Florida for the event.

We're a Maryland clan, so when David moved to Florida because of his job it was a big deal for us. Separation *within* the state was tolerated; separation by several states was unacceptable. Without a choice, though, we gave him, his wife, and new baby daughter a Maryland themed send-off at our Christmas party in 1984.

The distance between Maryland and Florida created a gap in our family. Our contact with Dave was much less than was usual for our family, which gathers regularly for a variety of events and holidays. As several years passed and a baby boy was born in 1988, we felt removed from the unfolding of Dave's marriage. Mom and stepfather Tom made several trips to visit; we looked at the snapshots, admired their new home, and gratefully received tidbits of news. But a cloud gathered many miles to our south, and we were barely aware of it.

When Dave arrived in 1990 for the wedding, we studied him with furtive alarm. He was thin and seemed tightly stressed. Preceding his visit, we had hints that his marriage was in trouble, so we attributed his appearance to that. The celebration of the moment obscured the ugly truth that revealed itself just below the surface. Besides—we didn't even know what we were looking at.

Our father, Rob, died from an apparent suicide in 1967. Since Dave was born in 1958, he only knew our dad for a mere nine years. Our father's death masked a demon in the closet that would not emerge for us until almost thirty years later in 1994. That demon would have a devastating link between father and son.

The reason for Dave's altered state that glorious May day was a rare genetic disease known as Huntington's that passes from parent to child with a chilling 50-50 chance of manifestation. Our father's intentional death hid the disease from us because he didn't live long enough to show the later stage indications and was never diagnosed. We can only surmise that he knew something was terribly wrong with him, and, being an avoider of doctors whom he never trusted, decided to end it rather than find out. Depression and suicide are common among Huntington's patients (both pre-symptomatic and diagnosed).

Over the years, I've sometimes experienced moments of realization when I see with clarity how life might have been different had my father not chosen to drive his car into a highway overpass. Eventually we would have discovered the disease in him, and my mother, in particular, would have been faced with agonizing years of caring for him. Huntington's takes a long time to kill you, typically fifteen to twenty years for the majority— although the younger manifestors (like Dave) die more quickly.

As for my father, we'll never know when he actually started to manifest or how long he would have lived. For David, we know he started to manifest sometime after moving to Florida, and we know he lasted until August 1999. He was 41-years-old when he died.

After the wedding in 1990, Dave's marriage dissolved into a nasty divorce based on misunderstood outbursts of temper, a typical by-product of Huntington's. When he was denied access to his children, his ex-wife didn't yet know the cause of his erratic behavior. She had much to learn about fear when David was diagnosed in 1994 after moving back to Maryland to be with family.

When the doctor at Johns Hopkins delivered the diagnosis, my mother and I were in the examining room with Dave. He accepted the verdict stoically, due in part probably to the damage already done to his mental faculties. The doctor told me sometime later that he considered Huntington's the cruelest of diseases because it robs you of both mind and body. Typical psychological manifestations are irritability, paranoia, and loss of judgment; typical physical manifestations are involuntary facial movements, unsteady gait, and speech impairment.

In 1872, John Huntington, a 22-year-old physician, a new graduate from Columbia University, first described Huntington's Disease accurately. His observations of multiple generations of a Long Island family led him to the conclusion that what he was studying was an unstoppable neurodegenerative affliction that caused certain parts of the brain to waste away.

With five children in our family and the youngest gone, the remaining four of us silently speculated about the odds of only one child being afflicted. It took a while, but we were to discover that the odds were indeed cruel. Carl, the third oldest after my sister and me, also inherited the flawed gene. Even though I've made much of Dave's distance from us in Florida, Carl lived right under our noses all his life and still we didn't know when he started to manifest. It starts so silently, so stealthily.

Looking back, it seems to us that we overlooked symptoms for many years, but we attributed unexplainable quirks to his 'artistic,' alternative lifestyle. Even his wife (his second) allowed years to drift by without questions. Childless and introverted, he remained on the sidelines of the family. When we finally acknowledged the truth and the hospital confirmed it, Carl's slow deterioration began in earnest.

It seemed strange to us that David, the youngest, would be the first claimed by Huntington's. It took until fairly recently for me to understand that the mutant defects (known as CAG repeats on chromosome 4) actually increase as the gene is passed down, meaning that Dave had more repeats and therefore earlier onset than Carl. Birth order matters.

When Carl died at 62-years-old in November of 2011, he was the oldest survivor of Huntington's in our family. Our paternal grandfather, who died of a heart attack at 52 before Huntington's could claim him, goes as far back as we can trace this pattern. Since the disease never skips a generation and our paternal grandmother lived to an old age without the disease, the link goes back to Carl Conrad Ruhl—our brother's namesake. Our father Robert died one week shy of turning 48.

Doctors at Johns Hopkins Hospital tell us that Huntington's is not a sex-linked disease, meaning that females and males have an equal chance of inheriting. In our family, though, it has traveled its ugly path from grandfather to son to grandson to grandson.

A genetic test to determine whether or not a person has Huntington's was devised in 1993 just prior to Dave's diagnosis. Before this breakthrough, clinical indicators were the only basis for diagnosis. It's a simple test, but there's nothing simple about getting the results. A positive result is a death warrant, carrying with it the burden of years of deterioration.

We three remaining sisters, deprived of brothers, are bonded by our survivorship. It's as if we stood at some cosmic roulette wheel and came away winners—not by bravery or volition but by invisible cellular chance.

Toward the end of Dave's life, when we had to resort to placing him in a nursing facility, my sister Chris and I went to visit him one sunny day. Tottering on his thin, erratic legs, Dave emerged from the inside of the building into the glory of the day outside. A grin spread across his face as he declared loudly, "It's a *great* day to be alive." My sister's eyes met mine behind his back. We'll never forget that moment, and from time to time I'm sure she (like me) steps out into welcoming sunshine and repeats his words with a catch in her throat.

"But now I saw clearly that life and time were like the readings of a seismograph; that life flowed—or careened, or plummeted, or soared, or perhaps merely slogged— forward from a series of spasms or shocks, as clearly traceable as the activity of a series of quakes. And that it was entirely possible, many years later, to look

back and see just where each quake had occurred and what sort of tracery it left . . . or what sort of damage. It was a frightening concept . . . that I was and forever would be vulnerable to the random spasms of my life, great or small."

from *Colony* by Anne Rivers Siddons

Brother Carl Ruhl (1949-2011)
holds newborn brother David Ruhl (1957-1999)

"It's so unfair that we should die,
just because we are born."

Anna Magnani, Italian actress

Storm Warnings

The glass has been falling all the afternoon,
And knowing better than the instrument
What winds are walking overhead, what zone
Of gray unrest is moving across the land,
I leave the book upon a pillowed chair
And walk from window to closed window, watching
Boughs strain against the sky

And think again, as often when the air
Moves inward toward a silent core of waiting,
How with a single purpose time has traveled
By secret currents of the undiscerned
Into this polar realm. Weather abroad
And weather in the heart alike comes on
Regardless of prediction.

Between foreseeing and averting change
Lies all the mastery of elements
Which clocks and weatherglasses cannot alter.
Time in the hand is not control of time,
Nor shattered fragments of an instrument
A proof against the wind; the wind will rise,
We can only close the shutters.

I draw the curtains as the sky goes black
And set a match to candles sheathed in glass
Against the keyhole draught, the insistent whine
Of weather through the unsealed aperture.
This is our sole defense against the season;
These are the things that we have learned to do
Who live in troubled regions.

Adrienne Rich

Vienna Waits for You

*It isn't until you come to a spiritual understanding of
who you are—not necessarily a religious feeling, but deep down,
the spirit within—that you can begin to take control.*

Oprah Winfrey

Going to sacred places is a bit uncomfortable for me.
Visiting shrines compels me not, and when there, I feel the
misfit.

Coming from a line of dedicated Lutherans, I'd probably be a
churchgoer by most odds, but somehow religion missed the mark
with me. My paternal grandparents were conservative German-
Americans who never missed church on the sabbath; my father
earned perfect attendance pins for twelve years running. Some things
just can't be explained, and although I've tried to interpret why for
many years, on the day of my confirmation, I cried.

I attended preparatory classes in anticipation of my first holy
communion. Little of the experience remains in memory, but I do
have a subconscious feeling of awkwardness; the ministers were
kind, but I failed the molding. The Saturday night before the
confirmation of my group to the congregation, I lay sleepless in my
twin bed, trying hard to deny the nothingness I felt. Surely I was
supposed to feel some manifestation of holiness or at least some
joyful anticipation of passing into the adult community from
childhood. The truth is, I discovered for the first time that I was a
non-believer. I was certain that if God did exist, he would strike me
dead as punishment before morning.

I wrestle with this still. It marks you as a bit strange not to
believe in the teachings of an established church.

Sometimes being away from home causes you to ponder some of the big questions about being human, and by extension, about being mortal.

This year I had the chance to travel farther for work, outside the continental U.S. I'm so tantalized by the possibilities abroad that I feel some days as if I'm holding my breath for the next email invitation. Certainly I still anticipate jobs in the States (one of my favorite jobs was in Brooklyn), but the window of opportunity has grown larger and fuller. Each trip requires me to perform— after all, I'm being paid to be a consultant— but each trip also offers personal extensions only limited by my imagination.

Hawaii was assigned to me in the spring of 2012. Having never been, the prospect was delicious, especially because it involved island hopping from Maui to the Big Island to Oahu. I always thought that I didn't really need to see either Hawaii or Alaska, but now I'm aghast that I was so wrong.

It was a second trip, though, one to Vienna, that prompts my reflections. Curiously, just a week before leaving for Vienna, I discovered the Billy Joel song "Vienna Waits for You."

In 1713, the Black Plague spread across Vienna. Emperor Charles VI made a vow that if the plague left the city, he would build a church dedicated to his namesake, St. Charles Borromeo (a 16th century Italian bishop famous for ministering to plague victims). His prayers were answered, and so he ordered the construction of Karlskirche (German for St. Charles Church) in 1715. The completion of the building took more than twenty years. The Baroque design integrates architectural elements from ancient Greece and Rome, making it a bit of an unconventional curiosity. The green copper dome rises 236 feet high, a recognizable landmark of the Viennese skyline.

I know that dome with some intimacy since I climbed to the top of it. Fortunately there's a glass-encased lift that takes you partway up the dome, but you must climb flights of steps to the top. By far the most acrophobic experience of my travels, it surpassed the spatial discomfort of looking down from high outdoor places.

Even the handrails provided little comfort as I made my way up the stairs, which felt detached and precarious despite their sturdy construction. There was disconcerting movement caused by not only my ascent, but by the descent of another person from above. I lost heart at one point and sat on the steps, gripping the rail in panic, preparing to turn back. I thought of contestants I'd seen on The Amazing Race and doubled my empathy for the stunts demanded of them. I told myself (aloud) that these were just steps, and I chanted the step count as I continued. It wasn't such a big deal, but it seemed so at the time.

Panting, more from fear than from exertion, I craned my neck upward to see the painting in the dome. Could it possibly equal the gorgeous frescoes I'd climbed past on the way up? If I were the religious type, I'd swear I saw heaven up there. The goldenness of the ring of cherubic angels gazing down upon you is stunning. As I consider myself a spiritual type instead, I'll leave it at saying it touched my soul.

Can the intensity of my experience be explained by appreciation of beauty? One would be without senses not to value the glory of the art contained in Karlskirche. The dedication required by devoted believers to create such a masterpiece challenges the boundaries of comprehension. It's more than art appreciation, surely. Although I've differed with the Catholic Church (since birth, by osmosis—probably!), it didn't matter that this church reveres things that aren't a part of me. It does matter that my humanness was connected to another time and place in which others strove, as I strive, to find meaning.

The counterpart to Karlskirche was my visit to Seegrotte. If Heaven is to be found up, the discovery of Hell must be down. Two hundred feet below the surface will suffice for me.

Seegrotte began as a 19th century gypsum mine dug out by eighty miners over the course of decades. (No, I didn't know what gypsum was until it was explained to be a mineral used in fertilizers.) Once a well was drilled in 1848, discovering gypsum close to the surface, the digging began. In 1912, an explosion caused the mine to flood, creating the largest subterranean lake in

Europe. The mine was rendered useless, but once the caves were re-discovered by cave explorers in the 1930's, they opened to the public. During World War II, the caves became the production site for Nazi jet fighters, eliminating exposure to bombing attacks. After World War II, the mine eventually became a tourist attraction.

Descending into the mine seemed the opposite of ascending the church dome, and it was intimidating as well. Even the cheerful narrations by our tour guide—a Himalayan man he called himself—failed to dispel the claustrophobic gloom of the march farther and farther into the old mine. We passed a grotto containing a shrine to the Virgin Mary cut into the wall. Miners lit candles there and prayed they would once again see the light outside. I think most of us felt tempted to pick up a votive and light it for luck, just in case.

One 'room' cut into the rock had once housed the horses needed to pull the gypsum-laden wagons. One detail was particularly unsettling: the horses were intentionally blinded to reduce their anxiety before their first entrance into the darkness of the mine where they would labor until they were no longer useful. This animal cruelty was a precursor to the human cruelty next revealed. When the Luftwaffe wished to produce new single-engine jet fighters (proposed to be flown by Hitler youths because pilots were becoming scarce as the war wore on), the mine turned into a subterranean factory. We passed another 'room' containing a display of fuselage assembly for the Heinkel 'People's Fighter', horrified to discover that the Nazis imported laborers from a nearby concentration camp, mortified to imagine the suffering that took place there.

In strange juxtaposition to the preceding discoveries, we came upon a large movie poster attached to the wall advertising the 1993 Disney film The Three Musketeers which was filmed, in part, at Seegrotte. A remnant of the filmmaking remains: a golden buccaneer's ship, a glamorized model in sharp contrast to its tomb-like surroundings, floats nearby. We embarked upon the many-chambered lake in a flat-bottomed skiff. (I discovered afterward that the boat ride had been suspended for some time after the drowning of several tourists in 2004, who became trapped under their boat once it capsized. The description of the current boat ride on the same tourist website where I got this information claimed it to be 'a quiet and romantic' getaway. Hardly!)

The visit to Seegrotte was fascinating but haunting. Glimpses of hell on Earth aren't easy to forget.

Growing up, I don't remember much fire-and-brimstone talk about Hell. The promise of heavenly delights far outnumbered threats of a sinner's fate. Even quite young, the talk about Heaven seemed fanciful to me, and I was often surprised by the storybook quality of the details. Streets lined with gold? Cherubs floating among clouds? I learned eventually, though, how devoutly most people profess to believe in an actual, physical paradise beyond this mortal existence. Eulogies asking congregants to imagine the deceased residing joyfully in Heaven make me squirm. I'm sure my denial of an afterlife seems inconceivable to some, but their wishfulness seems just as inconceivable to me.

I identified myself as a Lutheran until about sixteen. For a period of time after that, my father (who had decided to break with the Lutheran Church) took us to various other churches in search of something. In those mental ramblings you sometimes have when you imagine being re-united with a long-gone relative, I always wish I could ask him why he began to search and what he sought. What disenchanted him I'll never know. Leaving the liturgical and sacramental practices of the Lutheran church (baptism and communion in particular) didn't bother me at all. As I've said, my personal emotional break with the teachings of the church had already happened.

Eventually, after a couple of years I think, our family (minus my older sister Janet who had married) joined the Unitarian Church of Baltimore. Although the church is an elegant, historic landmark in the city, my strongest recollection of it was catching the glimmers of multiple, recessed ceiling lights in my newly-acquired engagement ring at the tender age of eighteen. The sermons were stimulating and highbrow, but I spent a number of air-headed Sundays mesmerized by the facets in my precious diamond. In hindsight, I realize how disappointed my new Protestant in-laws must have been that their only son married in such a 'peculiar' church (not architecturally peculiar at all, but the congregation didn't believe in the trinity, for Heaven's sake!)

Come to think of it, I baffled both of my husbands with my unconventional attitudes about religion. My first and only in-laws probably tolerated my alternative views because I was a teacher in training and my family seemed otherwise normal and respectable. My first husband was too hedonistic to bother much with talk from a pulpit. Because my second husband's parents had died before we met, he was on his own Methodist island against my religious skepticism and indifference. We didn't go to church; he wasn't comfortable in mine and I wasn't comfortable in his. I know I denied him something he valued, but he loved me enough to let it go.

And my children . . . set adrift in a world without a grounding in traditional religion? They've been by-passed by so many religious references in life because their Unitarian Sunday School classes spent more time making kites than reading the Bible. Karen once insisted on attending a Young Life weekend that she refused to believe would be religious, as I suggested it would be. When she hopped into my car after delivery back to her school's parking lot on Sunday evening, she admitted that I had been right, and yes, she was uncomfortable most of the time. "They kept talking about this Pontius guy," she reported. Jeff seems unable to grasp what it is I *do* believe in and has at times sidestepped identifying my religion to prospective dates.

Long past the self-consciousness of youthful conformity, they could choose to make religion a part of their lives, but so far I haven't seen signs of it. Neither of them was baptized, but if that should ever become an issue for either of them, a remedy could be made. My grandchildren get their religious exposure from other relatives, and they know intuitively that Mama Baer shies away from talk about God. There are many paths open to them. Perhaps I have yet to see religious connections through them that I haven't imagined.

It feels uncomfortable to be a secularist these days in America. The worry over JFK's Catholicism in the 60's seems mild compared to the charges by a sizable minority that Barack Obama is a Muslim in our midst today. And now we head deep into an election in which a Mormom wants to be President. The sting of disapproval from conservative Christians can be ferocious. Overt demonstrations of faith have become as obligatory as American flag lapel pins. The mixing of religion and politics is tough for me. I *want* to have courageous conversations about it, but such talk always feels forbidden.

Traveling isn't a luxury for me any longer; it's necessity. It stokes the fires of wonderment in me and subdues the fears of aging. The climb to the dome of a church far from home, the descent into a cave formerly unknown—each opportunity opens me to another piece of a miraculously complex world. How important is it to experience intense (yet momentary) emotional bonding with people who live and think differently? Like oxygen.

It's as if I'm sitting around a huge table filled with a jigsaw puzzle of the world. One-by-one, I pick up a piece, find its location, hover over a unique empty space, gently ease the angles into place, admire the discovery, and nod knowingly. A case in point: I grew up listening to German/Austrian composers. I can hum most of "Tales of the Vienna Woods" by Johann Strauss, but it wasn't until I drove through the Wienerwald that I connected it in time and space. When the tour guide referred to the Vienna Woods as the 'green lungs' of Vienna, I understood at last the rejunevation the Viennese feel when they escape their urban ways into those forested highlands. That's not to say that vicarious experience isn't wonderful, but there's magic in immersion. The combination of my childhood exposure to the waltz coupled with a visit to the place of its inspiration was sublime.

I want it said at my funeral that I was generous and joyful. I'm working on the generous part. And so, will there be an afterlife for me? I often feel unexplainable connections to those I've lost: Mom often seems to tap me on the shoulder with her cheerful 'rise and shine,' Larry often seems to bestow his benevolent presence upon me. If afterlife is not actual physical survival but is instead a spiritual lingering, that's fulfilment enough, it seems to me. After I die, what will remain of me, I wonder. It would be great to have a preview. My mother would have loved to know in advance that her three daughters would forever celebrate her optimism.

What quirks, what expressions, what likes and dislikes will my children and their children (and others who love me) recall about me in jest? What advice or observation I've made will cause one of them to try a little harder or hurt a little less? All those moments of unexpected transcendence, sometimes prompted by a sound or a glance, will be my afterlife. Will my life inspire someone after me in small ways? Without that hope, death would seem much more daunting.

Vienna Waits For You

Slow down, you crazy child
You're so ambitious for a juvenile
But then if you're so smart, tell me
Why are you still so afraid?

Where's the fire, what's the hurry about?
You'd better cool it off before you burn it out
You've got so much to do and only so many hours in a day.

But you know that when the truth is told
That you can get what you want or you can just get old
You're gonna kick off before you even get halfway through
When will you realize, Vienna waits for you?

Slow down, you're doing fine
You can't be everything you want to be before your time
Although it's so romantic on the borderline tonight, tonight

Too bad but it's the life you lead
You're so ahead of yourself that you forgot what you need
Though you can see when you're wrong, you know
You can't always see when you're right, you're right

You've got your passion, you've got your pride
But don't you know that only fools are satisfied?
Dream on, but don't imagine they'll all come true
When will you realize, Vienna waits for you?

Slow down, you crazy child
And take the phone off the hook and disappear for awhile
It's all right, you can afford to lose a day or two
When will you realize, Vienna waits for you?

Steps up into the dome of Karlskirche, 2012

"Laufen und Springen ist Lebensgefahrlich!
Schreien ist uncool!"

Translation: Running and jumping is life threatening!
Screaming is uncool!

(Sign at base of steps)

Letting It Out

"For women, the best aphrodisiacs are words. The G-spot is in the ears. He who looks for it below there is wasting his time."

Isabel Allende, author

"Guys would sleep with a bicycle if it had the right color of lip gloss on. They have no shame. They're like bull elks in a field."

Tori Ames, songwriter

I was young and unmarried when I lost my virginity. (Funny how that doesn't sound shocking anymore.) He was daring and I was naïve. I'd be lying, though, if I didn't admit that it was purely consensual. When I think back on it, I'm forced to acknowledge that good advice, good education, and good genes are just short of powerless in the face of lust. I wanted to be adored. A female will do anything to get that reassurance. Clever guys know that.

Because I wed at nineteen, I've always thought my underdeveloped exploratory phase with dating and sex led to my failure with monogamy in that first marriage.

Despite pride in my reasoning abilities . . . I must confess at last that the one part of my life over which I've had little understanding is my sexuality. I've hidden it, denied it, lied about it, buried it, and romanticized it. I'm sure I'm not finished figuring it out.

Few women of the 50's discovered what they really had between their legs. (Thank you, *Mad Men*, for allowing me to see that I wasn't an aberration.) It was all mystery. I didn't even know I had a clitoris. Looking back, it almost seems accidental that I got as much pleasure out of sex as I did.

I hope the younger females in my life enjoy their physical selves sooner than I did (and for the right reasons). I got tangled up in illusions too much, afraid to show the unrestrained side of me. I bought the Barbie and Ken version of sex too completely.

Before I go any further, let me say that with the exception of a midshipman who wanted nothing more than to date rape me in a closet at a party at the Naval Academy, all of the potential and actual sexual partners I've had in my life were (I think) considerate of me. Despite the fact that females generally believe they have a corner on the market of suffering (inconsiderate lovers, dull-witted spouses), the men in my life have cared about my happiness—sexually and emotionally. Even the most hedonistic among them seemed to care that I was satisfied.

I guess what I've finally found out is that you have to discover what you need sexually—even if layers of screwed-up thinking hide it—and savor it. Raised German and modest, it took me a long time to unearth it. I'm thrilled that I've had partners who knew, for the most part, how to have good sex and that in this late stage I've found a partner who listened well to women who talked about what pleasures them.

I had to compete with Ann Margret. My granddaughter has to compete with Taylor Swift. It never ends. The sex symbols of our lives set an impossible standard we fantasize about, and in the end, we hope someone will find us desirable. I've been amazingly lucky that despite all my real and imagined shortcomings, as Sophia Loren said, "Sex appeal is 50 percent what you've got and 50 percent what people think you've got."

Helen Gurley Brown, the editor of Cosmopolitan magazine from 1965 to 1997, died this August. I'm sure young women didn't take note and probably don't even recognize her name. In 1962, she authored a shocking little book titled Sex and the Single Girl, three decades before Sex and the City. I regret that I didn't take notice of it when it came out; it might have done me a world of good. I was so conventional at the time. Like many of Cosmo's target readers before Ms. Brown shook things up, I was more concerned with how to make a Jell-O salad than how to be alluring.

It's very suggestive to find the most recent issue of Cosmo placed deliberately on your bed stand as I did when I visited Matt for the first time. Although the magazine features women half my age and becomes repetitively predictable ("25 Sex Moves He Secretly Wishes You'd Try"), it is a guilty little pleasure.

I wasn't even a Cosmo reader until after Ms. Brown left the editorship, but in honor of her memory, I bought the September issue soon after reading her obituary. (Didn't know who the cover model Lucy Hale is until I looked her up, but there was that familiar cover teaser "The Naughty Orgasm Trick Couples Love.")

The New York Times declared that Helen was ninety when she died "though parts of her were considerably younger." They went on to describe her as "A tiny, fragile-looking woman who favored big jewelry, fishnet stockings and minidresses till she was well into her 80s." She considered herself a feminist but was called to task by a number of notable women over the years for views that contradicted enlightened thinking about women's roles. She flaunted her advocacy of using sexual favors for personal advancement. ("Good Girls Go to Heaven/Bad Girls Go Everywhere.")

Brown's *Sex and the Single Girl* seems quaint now, but I think it's amusing that it fits me now in my later life better than it did when published. Since my widowhood in 2005, I've become the single I never gave myself a chance to be in the 60's. There's such freedom that comes with prioritizing your own needs, especially the sexual ones.

In her book *Prime Time*, Jane Fonda addresses intimacy boldly in what she calls The Third Act. She refers to her own preparations "for some loving" as an older woman, understanding full well that it might not come along. Like me, she found a caring, sensual partner and discovered that there's fulfillment in being "a free-standing, self-validated" woman who no longer wants to be "entwined and needy."

At our age, my partner and I could easily allow companionship to replace romance, but we want more. Passion comes easily when you have plenty of time and no one else to look after. I've made no secret of my choice to remain single and live separately. We've made a commitment to monogamy and the safety that comes with it, and both of us strive to keep sexuality alive and well between us.

It's hard to explain to my daughter, nieces, and granddaughter how different expectations have become for women of my generation. Never did I imagine as a girl bride that I would become a woman in her sixties with a thriving libido.

The luckiest outcome for me sexually is that throughout my life I haven't been damaged by it, especially considering the potential for damage is immense. Nothing makes you more vulnerable than your physical self. Raised on the need to please makes me particularly susceptible to this kind of damage. I can't say how liberating it is to accept pleasure and to love my body for the service it has rendered. After years and years of berating myself for not being perfect physically, I accept the gift of being okay.

Respect your body. Take care of it, but share it with those you can trust. That's a tall order and fraught with many dangers, but believe in the amazing deliverance of lying naked to the world, your lover, and to yourself.

"Flesh goes on pleasuring us, and humiliating us,
right to the end."

Mignon McLaughlin, journalist

Hyatt Regency Maui Resort and Spa, Hawaii, 2012

*"Whatever else can be said about sex,
it cannot be called a dignified performance."*

Helen Lawrenson, writer

Love Me Like A Man

The men that I've been seeing
They got their soul up on a shelf
You know they could never love me
When they can't even love themselves

And I want someone to love me
Someone who really understands
Who won't put himself above me
Who just love me like a man

I never seen such losers darling
Even though I tried
To find a man who can take me home instead of
Taking me for a ride
And I need someone to love me
Darling I know you can
Don't you put yourself above me
You just love me like a man

They all want me to rock them
Like my back ain't got no bone
I want a man to rock me
Like my backbone was his own

Darling I know you can
Believe it when I tell you
You can love me like a man

Came home sad and lonely
I feel like I wanna cry
Want a man to hold me
Not some fool who'll ask me why
And I need someone to love me
Baby you can
Don't you put yourself above me
Just love me like a man

Bonnie Raitt

Al's Body Shop

Dream like you'll live forever; Live like you'll die today.

I believe in regular tune-ups. It's been so ingrained in me to take care of what I have that it became unthinkable years ago not to brush my teeth before going to bed, not to change bed sheets regularly, not to get my hair cut on a schedule. It's all part of a control freak's chemistry. People like me are convinced that deliberate, planned actions guard us against the random wackiness of life.

And that's why I ended up at Al's Body Shop on August 31, 2011.

To be precise, I was actually at an Ellicott City hair salon—gawking, frozen-to-the-spot, staring at a parking space at 3711 Columbia Pike. My hair stylist (apparently observing me) finally opened the salon door, intrigued by my delayed entrance. "You are coming in, aren't you?" she inquired with an amused smirk.

The object of my fascination was an end parking space once occupied for a three-month period by a blue Oldsmobile belonging to my first husband. The details have faded. Sometime during the 70's and for some reason that escapes me, his car needed some bodywork. Any savvy Ellicott City resident knew the best man to go to—Albert Baer. If he laid hands on your damaged car, all traces of injury disappeared beneath his expert touch. Tucked behind Taylor's Department Store on Columbia Pike, Al's Body Shop was almost unfindable unless you knew exactly where you were going. Your first glimpse of it was a shock; dingy, unchanged by any attempt at 'sprucing up,' the grey cinderblock warehouse defied any clean-clothed person to exit unsmudged. Every inch was blackened by a timeless grunge generated by innumerable vehicles whose dark fluids—oil and gasoline—permeated every surface. Dismembered parts of cars and trucks littered about, their usefulness catalogued no doubt in the mind of the astute owner. Generous and playful with most of his customers, Al could be downright irascible if he didn't care for you.

Al had no use for my first husband, a high school schoolmate known for being overindulged by his parents and therefore scorned as spoiled. If Al didn't like you, your car repair could take a long time. Despite his repeated, pathetic attempts to deliver Al's coffee just as he liked it, my husband was powerless to get his car out of that parking space and into Al's shop, week after week after week.

And so I stood in front of Ooh la Lal (not a misspelling; the owner's last name is Lal) on a brilliant late-summer morning, transfixed by memory. The salon opened a year ago, the third business to launch itself there on Columbia Pike since Al's death in 2001.

The former interior of the building has been erased; who would believe this trendy, stylish enterprise could occupy the same space. Bent fenders have been replaced with shampoo stations. A Betty Boop statute teases you inside the red double doors. It's all New York black-and-white with images of Marilyn and Audrey. There is one way to get a telltale glimpse of the former no-nonsense building under the glitz; poke your head around the corner of the outside deck and look at the exterior sidewall. Oh, yeah. It's still ugly.

After my divorce from husband #1, I married Larry Baer and became Albert Baer's sister-in-law. This gave me claim to answer the curious questions of the people who work at Ooh la Lal. Why curious? There lies the tale. Al Baer has become the most popular ghost in town.

> *Angels, and ministers of grace, defend us!*
> *Be thou a spirit of health, or goblin damn'd*
> *Bring with thee airs from heaven, or blasts from hell*
> *Be thy intents wicked or charitable*
> *Thou com'st in such a questionable shape*
> *That I will speak to thee.*

> Hamlet Act I, Scene 4

It's quite understandable that folks in Shakespeare's day would believe in the supernatural; so much about life was still a mystery.

Curious, though, with science answering so many questions in the past couple of centuries, that paranormal beliefs remain so strong. Fully 90% of Americans say they believe in paranormal experiences (which takes into account ESP, ghosts, UFOs, etc.) People *want* to believe. The human brain is always trying to determine why things happen.

We outgrew myths of old, and for the most part, we don't blame mischief on fairies or elves anymore, but the unexplainable still tugs at us—even though most religions try to dissuade the superstitious and their supernatural thinking. Also interesting is that paranormal beliefs appear to have little relation to individuals' education levels. College students as well as high school dropouts confess to surveyors that they believe.

In 2005 CBS News surveyed a random sample of 808 Americans, of whom 48% said they believe in ghosts, and 22% said they have personally seen or felt the presence of a ghost. In the same year, the Gallup Poll surveyed 1,721 people; 40% said they believe in haunted houses.

Ghostly manifestations to the living include an interesting array of things: spectral appearances, unexplainable movement of items, noticeable smells, sounds such as moans, touch sensations. Since Al Baer's sudden death from a heart attack while working in his body shop more than a decade ago, reports of his presence in the building abound. The first tenants in the building after his death, two partners in an antique business, were so bothered by Al's hauntings that they couldn't function properly. Reports of their experiences (which circulated rapidly) were picked up by the local press, and curiosity grew. Soon Al's widow and his two grown sons were well aware of all the talk. They were understandably shaken.

Eventually they'd had enough, and so Albert's youngest son paid a visit to the antique dealers. He dreaded walking back into his father's former place of business (and site of his death), but he was no doubt feeling protective of his father's memory. He gave no indication to the antique dealers of his identity and presented himself as a customer who had heard rumors. This son, as down-to-earth as a person can be, expected to hear nonsense. What he was told shook him; the two antique dealers described the ghost they'd seen in accurate detail, including tidbits no strangers could know. They reported objects missing and described sounds and strange sensations at length; neither of the men dared to enter the shop alone and so they corroborated each other's observations.

The antique dealers felt they had no recourse but to close up their business and move on. The next tenants didn't experience the same ghostly intensity, but they, too, reported strange happenings. The legend of Al Baer's ghost was solidly in place, and eventually his family began to accept it with good grace. Ghost tours of Ellicott City incorporated Al's Body Shop into their visits, and his story continues to be the most popular in town. My hair stylist, among others who currently work at Ooh La Lal, often recount their encounters with Al.

Ellicott City's reputation as a good ghost town stems from Lilburn, a home built by one Henry Hazelhurst in 1857 and purported to be haunted. The massive grey stone edifice of gothic design remains standing and occupied today, so residents and tourists are treated to the sight of its unusual appearance on College Avenue whenever they choose. I drive past it several times a week, my eyes always caught by its unusual parapet-topped tower. The house is shrouded in the sadness of the original owner, Mr. Hazelhurst, a prosperous Englishman, a sympathizer with the Confederacy. He insisted on remaining in his beloved house until his death in 1900, even after nearly a half-century of heartbreak in the house, including the death of three children and his wife. The original 2600-acre estate dwindled after the Civil War while Hazelhurst still lived, and then again after his death, but its dignity remains with the house and the seven acres upon which it sits.

After a fire gutted the house in the early 1900s, it was restored. The only obvious change during the restoration was in the rebuilding of the tower. Instead of duplicating the Gothic peaks, the new master of this eerie house created the parapets seen there today. The tower is the source of most of the ghost stories; the sound of Mr. Hazelhurst's footsteps (previously reported before the fire) grew more persistent. Stories of strange happenings spread throughout the town until townspeople were afraid to approach Lilburn.

Perhaps Al Baer isn't the only Baer brother to haunt a place he loved. Perhaps both Baer brothers have defied the finality of death. I have another tale to tell.

Two years after my husband Larry's death, I rented our weekend house near Gettysburg to a neighbor's brother who said he wanted the option to buy it. The house had been Larry's joy after his diagnosis of prostate cancer. He anticipated the clearing of the wooded lot in preparation for the construction as one who believed he would defy the odds. He had only several years to love it, but love it he did. Our son-in-law was our builder, making the enterprise all the sweeter. The weekends spent there kept us sane throughout the endless rounds of radiation and chemotherapy. Afterward, without Larry there, the house became a bittersweet reminder and lost its charm.

In the fall of 2008, after he had rented the house for over a year, my tenant (a gentle yet odd sort of fellow) sent me the strangest email I've ever received:

"I have to tell you about my experiences living in your house on Bluebird Trail. It appears all nice on the outside, but there is something wrong living there. Strange noises started mid-November in 2007 and continued to get worse from that time on. The low-frequency humming and noise, especially downstairs, got so bad I had to increase the volume of the TV to try to drown it out. Something or someone was either just not happy or was not happy that I was there and in time it became debilitating for me to live there. It was affecting me physically and mentally. I could not sleep unless I drank myself to sleep because of the noise. It reverberated in my inner ear constantly. As soon as I got to the house after work, I could hear it inside my car. This may sound bizarre, but it is my true experience. I have no reason to lie . . . I could never buy the place because of it. There is a very unhappy entity in that house and maybe you should have it exorcized by a good priest. I think Larry is still there."

I won't repeat my shocked reply, a mixture of alarm and misgiving (but not the reply of a believer in ghosts). It was uncomfortable for me to give up the house, knowing as I did how much it meant to Larry, compounded by the knowledge that he would not have liked my renter living there.

A return email arrived:

"I think Larry is stuck between our world and the light above, where he needs to go. I sense anger and resentment for all the years he worked to get the house and then to have it all gone before he could really enjoy it with you. I sense a great deal of love that he has for you but such total frustration that fate took him away. . . I told him I 'heard' him and know his struggle. I do not know what faith you live by, but you need to engage a worthy person to mitigate his release from this world and to go to the light. Please know that I tell you this for not only your own well-being but for Larry especially. He needs to be shown the way home now."

I sold the house not long after to a wonderful retired couple from Thurmont. The husband is from the same mold as Larry—handy, capable, caring. They have kept the house as he would have, and for that I'm so glad. I've driven by it a few times and have sat in my parked car across from it, flooded with emotion. I'll never know if they have experienced any unexplainable occurrences, but I trust not.

I'm becoming somewhat enamored of the possibility that I may return as a ghost. I like the idea. And after all, ghost believers include first ladies, queens, and prime ministers who have supported the ghost of Abraham Lincoln in The White House. Not all ghost believers skulk through Alcatraz or chant to Bloody Mary. Being one who stirs things up while alive, I see no reason why I shouldn't anticipate stirring things up after I'm dead. My rejection of an afterlife in heaven or hell shouldn't preclude the ghostly realm; I don't see why I shouldn't be free to express myself to those I've left behind. No matter how old I am when I die, I'll never feel that I finished all I wanted to do.

So let's make plans, shall we? If you should hear the rattling of some teacups, say, without any obvious cause, think of me as the culprit. If you start thinking about an idea for the Christmas party on the beach in July, I'm there. I'll be a polite ghost, I promise, but if I can give a poke every now and again, I will.

I think the supernatural is a catch-all for everything we don't understand about the vast other parts of life that we cannot perceive.

William Shatner

*"Remember that happiness is a way of travel . . .
not a destination."*

Roy M. Goodman, politician

The Trash Trilogy

"One must remember that there is such a thing as
good bad taste and bad bad taste."

John Waters

I will be forever grateful that the Broadway musical *Hairspray* swept the 2003 Tony Awards because it helped to ease a guilt-ridden aspect of my motherhood. Family is the heart of me, and so it is with pain that I finally confess to involving my daughter in an escapade so depraved as to seem unimaginable even after all these years.

Baltimore's outrageous native John Waters has become an international icon of bad taste. His pencil-thin mustache (originally styled in honor of Little Richard) is almost as familiar to Baltimoreans as the Natty Boh mustache. Since the release of his film *Polyester* in 1981, he has become mainstream, but he still resides in the hometown where he will always be an infamous treasure. Even after *Hairspray*'s huge success (first his screenplay in 1988, then Broadway, then a 2007 movie remake) he has remained true blue to his roots. Based on Baltimore's teenage dance party, *The Buddy Deane Show* (my girlhood obsession), *Hairspray* captured a whole chunk of my life, and I thank John Waters for that.

Born in Lutherville, a Baltimore suburb, in 1946, Waters grew up the son of comfortably affluent parents. From childhood he was a different kind of kid. Staging violent puppet shows for kids earned him pocket money, and he watched adult-only films through binoculars at the local drive-in. His favorite film was *The Wizard of Oz*. Waters says, "When they throw water on the witch she says 'Who would have thought a good little girl like you could destroy my beautiful wickedness.' That line inspired my life."

On his sixteenth birthday he got an 8mm movie camera from his grandmother that launched the rest of everything for him. He graduated from Boys' Latin and then went on to NYU 'for about five minutes' (he claims) because it was not edgy enough for him. He was caught smoking marijuana and was thrown out of his NYU dorm.

I must assume his parents were supportive and patient with him as he and his friends in Lutherville, especially Glenn Milstead (who went on to become Waters' most famous recurring film character Divine) became the Dreamlanders, the name for their early production company. Along with my husband and two children, I spent two gorgeous fall days in 1976 with the Dreamlanders at the Waters family home in Lutherville. Surreal in my memory still, those two days are a blur of tingling exposure to a life on the outer edge.

At twenty-six Waters became the much talked about writer and director of the film *Pink Flamingos*, released in 1972. Regardless of whatever else he does in his career, Waters will be eulogized as the man who created the last scene in that movie which set out to poke fun at censorship laws at the time. There's no delicate way to say it. In the final scene, a small dog defecates; Divine scoops it up and puts it in his mouth. In the long run, *Pink Flamingos* helped make trash film more respectable. My downfall was that I had only heard about the film but had never seen it. It wasn't until years later that I rented it with trepidation and watched it slack-jawed and horrified. When I first met John Waters, I fell under the spell of celebrity like Red Riding Hood did to the wolf.

Note: Only twice has renowned movie critic Roger Ebert refused to assign a star rating to a film: once for *Pink Flamingoes* and once for *The Human Centipede*. He explained that a movie made to disgust its viewers cannot be judged as good or bad. On the re-release of *Pink Flamingoes* for its 25th anniversary (restored for its revival), Ebert claimed that with any luck he wouldn't have to see it again for 25 years, and if he hadn't retired by then, he would.

Female Trouble followed *Pink Flamingoes* in 1974, and in 1976, the thirty-year-old 'local sensation' began the third film in what was to become his trash trilogy. The title of that film, *Desperate Living*, still curdles on my tongue even when I merely think it. My first husband and I thought ourselves rather a hot party ticket at the time among our friends in Ellicott City and had made the acquaintance of Bill Platt, a man with money who was about to help finance John Waters' new project. I can't recall the location or the circumstance, but he met our daughter Karen and suggested she'd be perfect for a small part, the child of the lead character. Karen's never-cut long hair and tiny stature must have somehow fit his idea for a small opening scene in which the neurotic movie-mother (played by actress Mink Stole) yells at her children for what she perceived as bad behavior.

Apparently a conversation transpired with John Waters, and we were asked if we were interested. Do I remember asking questions appropriate for any caring, concerned parent? Not at all. We were told when we'd be needed at Waters' parents' home (in a respectable Baltimore County neighborhood) and our anticipation built. Did I know Karen would play the daughter of a deranged character played by an actress named Mink Stole? Did I know she'd be part of 'a work of true trash art' as advertised on its VHS movie jacket? Stupidly, no. I never even asked to see a script.

The extent of my oblivion recently became clearer to me as I unearthed the old slides we took that day in 1976 and gazed at them through a small hand-held slide viewer in anticipation of digitizing them. For all these years since the filming, I've referred to meeting Divine and taking a picture of him/her (the aforementioned Glenn). *People* magazine described Divine as the Drag Queen of the Century. Imagine my chagrin to read that although Waters intended Divine to star in *Desperate Living*, he/she was unavailable because of a contractual tour as a cabaret singer. It was to be the only feature film Waters made without Divine prior to the actor's death at forty-two (obesity coupled with sleep apnea). Probably the film seemed doomed after another Waters regular, David Lochary, bled to death after accidentally cutting himself while on PCP just before production. Jean Hill (a relative unknown then and now) played the part of Grizelda Brown, maid to Peggy Gravel, movie-mother to my daughter Karen's character, Beth Gravel.

Desperate Living was released in May 1977, and we were invited to its premiere. All of Waters' films first showed at either the

Senator or Charles Theater in Baltimore, but I can't remember which one we sat in as invited guests. I add, hastily, that our children were *not* invited to the premiere. If they had been there and seen it, I would have died on the spot and never grown into a remorseful older woman. I think I only lasted about thirty minutes into the ninety-minute movie. Fleeing quietly but determinedly from the darkened theater, we were probably unnoticed.

Anyone familiar with moviemaking knows how tedious most of it is, and certainly the two days of filming we attended were no exception. There was only professional, carefully detailed working— none of which we saw except for a few brief shots done on the lawn outside. I have photos of the scene in which Karen is involved in outdoor baseball where her film brother accidentally hit the ball through a window, enraging their mother. We did not see the indoor filming of the scene in which Beth (Karen's part) and her pretend older brother Bosley are scolded by their mother for playing doctor. We were told there were several takes and that all went well. I didn't have a clue. I have to believe that if I'd seen the indoor shooting with Mink Stole shrieking, I would have realized what we'd gotten into and pulled the plug on the whole thing. But then, I'll never know. The entire production cost a paltry $65,000, including the sandwiches we were served for lunch and enjoyed with the cast and crew.

Desperate Living's plot is ludicrously raunchy. Peggy Gravel and her overweight maid go on the lam after Grizelda smothers Peggy's husband. The two are arrested by a cross-dressing policeman who gives them an ultimatum to go to jail or be exiled to Mortville, a filthy shantytown ruled by evil Queen Carlotta. Eventually Mortville's citizens overthrow Carlotta, kill her, roast her, and serve her pig-like on a platter with an apple in her mouth.

I've never seen the rest of the film after the arrest by the policeman. I tried to watch it once more after that original screening in 1977 by renting the movie from Blockbuster. I smuggled the bag home, waited until nobody was around and pushed Play. Mortified, I watched until I couldn't stand it anymore and returned it the same day.

Nothing can adequately describe my reaction to seeing my daughter's name listed under Cast in the article for *Desperate Living* in Wikipedia. On IMDb (Internet Movie Database) Karen's picture is blessedly missing from her cast listing. If you were to assume that I'm implying pleasure, you'd assume wrong. There it is—proof to the world that I allowed my child to work for the man whose one-man-show is titled *This Filthy World.*

I've always told Karen I hope she'll never see her movie. Curiosity being what it is, that seems unlikely, so I can only hope she laughs about it. Perhaps the loosening of movie standards in subsequent years (think *The Hangover* and *Bridesmaids*) makes the film less shocking, but its unpolished wince factor still stands. There are even clips from the film on YouTube. The actor's fee she was paid by check (signed by Waters) is framed and hangs in the home bar she and her friends refer to as Stewart's Bar & Grill. John Waters' accountant was probably annoyed for weeks when that check was never cashed.

Critics on Rotten Tomatoes give *Desperate Living* a 70% approval rating and audiences give it an 81%. (The handful of critics doesn't represent mainstream critics, of course. Janet Maslin of *The New York Times* described the film as "a pointlessly ugly movie that found high humor among low life.") I'm stupefied that this grotesque comedy amuses and pleases anyone. But then . . . I'm seeing it with the eyes of a mother.

One critic says, "John Waters' features *Female Trouble* (1974) and *Desperate Living* (1977) reinforced Waters' outlaw reputation with their satiric skewering of middle-class values and shattering of the suburban status quo. Reportedly, famous critic Rex Reed groaned (after viewing a Waters film), "Where do these people come from? Where do they go when the sun goes down?"

It's some small consolation to me that *Desperate Living* is the least known film of the Trash Trilogy. *Pink Flamingos* and *Female Trouble* are names frequently connected with Waters, but I've never encountered anyone short of a Waters devotee who references *Desperate Living.*

Also on that VHS movie jacket is the claim "Beware: This film contains nudity and outrageous sexual situations. The world may never be the same again." (I would add, "This movie is just plain disgusting!")

In his 1983 book *Crackpot*, Waters included a chapter titled 'Going to Jail' in which he says, "I decided to follow my father's advice that 'showbiz is never forever' and got my first real job. With a paycheck from the State of Maryland yet. Teaching, of all the peculiar things. Or in the jargon of the field, 'rehabilitating.' Criminals. Big ones. Now when strangers approach me to ask about Divine or my next film project, I could truthfully tell, 'Oh, I'm into corrections now'."

He taught his first class at the Patuxent Institution, located halfway between Baltimore and Washington. He claims he loved going to jail so much that he often arrived early for class. He gained acceptance, probably because of his nonjudgmental attitude toward the inmates. He told them, "Next time you feel like killing somebody, don't *do* it for God's sake—write about it, draw it, paint it." He startled them by admitting, "These films I make are my crimes, only I get paid for them instead of doing time."

He explained that he wanted to start off a class with a bang, so he decided to screen "one of my celluloid atrocities, *Desperate Living*, which may have been a mistake because the head of education had decided to come to the class." He had never seen a John Waters movie. When the visitor left, he told Waters that he didn't know whether to thank him or punch him. The student inmates all agreed that they would rather stay in jail than go to Mortville.

Perhaps I'll need an asterisk on my obituary. "Beware: Parents who step over the edge for a good look, may live to regret it." Those free-wheeling years in the 70's make me smile in many ways, but I'll always remember Waters' boast, "I pride myself on the fact that my work has no socially redeeming value."

Such trash talk!

"When you're unemployable, as I am, you have to think of ways to supplement your income. I barely made it through high school, can't type without looking at the keys, have such a low mechanical aptitude that plugging something in is difficult, would get into fist fights if I worked retail, and am a complete wimp at physical labor. All I can really do is blab."

John Waters

The Harlot of Hickory High

*For what do we live, but to make sport for our neighbors and
laugh at them in our turn?*

Jane Austen

T he famous Hatfield-McCoy feud ran off and on for nearly
thirty years. At the end of May this year, the History Channel
aired a three-part miniseries starring Kevin Costner about the
feud. Everybody I know was hooked on it.

In the condo where I've lived for six years, we all gather about
once every other month to socialize over drinks. The tradition started
in November 2006, about five months after the originals moved into
the newly built four story condo (part of Taylor Village—a
sprawling mix of homes, villa homes, and high rises that occupy
formerly pastoral acreage above Ellicott City). Sixteen units brought
strangers together to share their lives in the summer of 2006 (some
singles, some couples). The only required commonality is our ages—
we're the over fifty-five set—and the absence of children (unless
they're visiting). I'm on the first floor where only singles have lived
until recently; new neighbors, a minister and his wife, are now my
next-door neighbors.

On the night of May 30th, the third and final episode of
Hatfields and McCoys was airing at 9:00 pm, and since our parties
usually run from 7-9, the majority of residents said their goodbyes
and retired to their sofas. Judging by the conversation at our party,
most of them watched Devil Anse Hatfield and Randall McCoy
battle it out to a bitter end on the borders of Kentucky and West
Virginia.

Like most of my condo neighbors, I lived in a single home
surrounded by a lawn for most of my life, so communal living is our

later-stage lifestyle choice in an effort to simplify life. Certainly we all anticipated the plusses of two community pools, total exterior landscaping, and the assumption of like-minded neighbors. Most of us admit that downsizing was good for us and that cleaning less space is a relief. For me, condo living offered a way to put aside the burdens of home maintenance. Instinctively I craved the freedom to leave my dwelling whenever I chose without worrying about it while gone, and the assurance that it would be the same as I left it upon return.

Given my new widowhood, moving provided a spur to action that served me well. There was so much emotion tied to our house in Ellicott City and the weekend house we'd built in Fairfield, PA. A new place of my own allowed me to redefine myself as a single; it was significant that I be the first owner so I could define it. Truly I burrowed into it.

Meeting new people wasn't high on my list of reasons for moving. I was too focused on myself (and my survival as a single) to give much thought to my neighbors. I'm embarrassed to say that I hoped mostly that my neighbors would be clean and quiet. Self-absorption dominated after the trauma of all things connected to losing a husband, and I proceeded full speed ahead into making myself comfortable. It wasn't easy. Breaking apart twenty-five years of stuff and married habits is tough. I tackled the physicality of it unaware of how exhausting it would be. Not only was I pushing around a lot of boxes and furniture; I was learning to think with singleness—not the least of which was being entirely responsible for driving all the time.

As time passed the first year, I gradually learned the names of my Building #3 neighbors, although not nearly as quickly as I could have had I not been so self-absorbed. Meeting people at the elevator or the mailboxes had to translate into who was married to whom and what unit they lived in. Given that my spatial awareness is almost non-existent, it took forever to figure out who lived on the front of the building and who lived on the back. I'm one of three Kathys who must be identified by first and last name to avoid confusion. Sorting out names of grandchildren is a secondary (and still incomplete) endeavor among us.

Each of us could easily have a stereotypical nickname: the gourmet, the organizer, the nurturer, etc. One of my favorite friends here jokingly referred to me as the resident harlot. Considering that my boyfriend arrives some Friday nights (one of the few nights I remember to leave the porch light on) and departs on Sundays to my blown kisses, that seems fair enough. I actually relish the title. My numerous comings and goings with suitcases are easily observed (and *everything* is observed in a complex like ours). The frankness of my essays leaves little of my life unexposed, and I share most new adventures gleefully. Less conservative than most of my neighbors, I probably raise an eyebrow from time to time. All in all, we're a congenial bunch, known throughout the community as the fun building.

And there was Michele.

Coincidence brought us together; she bought Unit C, I bought Unit D. From the moment we discovered our mutual widowhood from prostate cancer, the die was cast. She was destined to tell me her life story and I to tell her mine. The enormous bonus was that she and I became a sisterhood of friendship, gradually sharing more and more of each other's lives until we told each other everything. My knock on her door or her knock on mine reassured both of us. We eventually had a silly ceremony of changing our seasonal door wreaths on the same day. Birthdays were moaned about; children were bragged about and worried over. We enjoyed the mutuality of trust and affection.

Whether she went on a trip or I did, the de-briefing of our times apart were thorough to the smallest detail. Since I travel a lot, she frequently collected my mail and reported missed community gossip upon my return. Her trips to her family in the Dominican Republic were special, and I delighted in hearing both about her girlhood there but also about how her family interacted with their American flyaway. Michele had met her future husband, a dashing young man in uniform, on the Staten Island ferry while visiting the states with her mother. They were married while each hardly understood the language of the other. She never lost her Spanish accent, which sometimes confused servers when we dined out together.

Fifteen years my senior, Michele sometimes became my adviser as well as my confidante. Her wise, carefully considered opinion of world events sometimes tempered my liberal shoot-from-the-hip views. She cooled my tirades against Sarah Palin and reminded me of the other side to gun control. Growing up under Trujillo gave her a perspective on politics that I respected and sought. Watching her preside over her family (and our condo) as the queen bee amused me. She was the center of all things social, organizing countless games of cards. Our first all-condo gathering was her doing, and the two of us often spearheaded subsequent gatherings. Always the lady, she oozed old-world charm and graciousness. Sometimes people sit up straighter and watch their grammar around me, but Michele had that effect on me. Norman Rockwell would have illustrated us as two proper matrons sipping tea and eating scones, but fire burned beneath our exteriors. Passionate about not giving in to aging, both of us got up each day with the intention of doing something interesting (and maybe even fun). She was my unexpected blessing of Hickory High.

I underestimated the adjustments required for communal living when I moved in. I recently read, "The world is full of small ignorances. We must all do our best to ignore them and thereby keep them small." Sharing space means the possibility of multiple slights and misunderstandings. Parking spaces (not assigned but used on a first-come basis) have turned out to be an issue around here, and the only two frictions I've had with neighbors were caused by cars (or in one of the two cases, a truck). These reminded me how easily a small thing can turn into a big thing. Like the Hatfield-McCoy feud, perceived wrongs can escalate into ugly stuff. None of us wants to be uneasy around our neighbors, so the delicate balances are given much attention.

A few times I've wished I could go back to dealing with just my own peculiarities, surrounded by an acre of ground, but most of the time I've been damn glad to have good neighbors very near who had my back. Especially Michele. Never have I been so glad that my boldness was returned with warmth and love. We were special friends because there were no boundaries, and she loved the harlot in me.

For our last Christmas together, Michele sent me a card. On it she wrote, 'What a lucky day when I met you.' It was indeed.

Don't ever take a good neighbor for granted.

In memory of
Michele Abel
1930-2011

Suburban sprawl – Maryland 1973

"The cities will be part of the country; I shall live 30 miles from my office in one direction, under a pine tree; my secretary will live 30 miles away from it too, in the other direction, under another pine tree. We shall both have our own car. We shall use up tires, wear out road surfaces and gears, consume oil and gasoline. All of which will necessitate a great deal of work ... enough for all."

Le Corbusier, The Radiant City (1967)

Matt Goes Down
(on a Little Asian Lady)

I haven't been everywhere, but it's on my list.

Susan Sontag

Few words are as expressive as 'luggage.' It says what it is without any trace of euphemism. Having been raised on polite substitutions for blunt words, I notice when a word declares its honesty. Take the word 'scar,' for example. It doesn't fool around like 'blemish' does. For a traveler, luggage tells it like it is.

To lug something is to drag or pull something laboriously. Despite the shift to wheeled luggage in recent years, and even with the trend toward four-wheeled spinner luggage, it's still a matter of hauling around your stuff in an annoying container that often makes you a bit crazy.

George Carlin had a famous stand-up routine about Stuff.

"Sometimes you leave your house to go on vacation. And you gotta take some of your stuff with you. Gotta take about two big suitcases full of stuff, when you go on vacation. You gotta take a smaller version of your house. It's the second version of your stuff . . . And even though you're far away from home, you start to get used to it, you start to feel okay, because after all, you do have some of your stuff with you."

The amount of stuff you decide to lug along with you has consequences, not the least of which is that most airlines charge you to haul it. (And why *shouldn't* they? If you think pulling your luggage up to the ticket counter is bad, try talking to baggage handlers for a few minutes.) Heavy packers have to consider that even generous Southwest charges $50 if your bag tips the scale above 50 pounds.

My real beef is with carry-on luggage. The most scorned (and ignored) apparatus in any airport is the device that says "If your carry-on does not fit into this, it must be checked through with the airline." To this day, I've never seen anyone test his or her bag for size in one of those contraptions. You must regularly contend with travelers who stretch the limits of 'carry-on' to absurd lengths. I've seen some people (particularly women) carry on the equivalent of a Target store—all while balancing a super-sized Coke and a smelly hoagie. And how about those who bring a full-sized pillow with them?

Anyway . . . deciding what stuff to pack is no fun, re-packing it to go home is even worse, and in general I'm completely jealous of the twenty-somethings who cruise through airports with a North Face backpack, earbuds in place, hands free to navigate their smartphones. I travel for business as well as pleasure, and that means I often don't have a choice about what to pack. The most complicated packing of all involves combining a pleasure trip with a business trip, in which case you're screwed no matter what.

In July of 2011, I was booked to present a workshop for The College Board's AP Annual Conference in San Francisco. Matt and I decided to extend the trip with a visit to a former student of mine living in Menlo Park and a visit with his best friend living in Fresno. The logistics of packing for such a trip induced agitation for days.

For Matt, the biggest challenge is his shoes. Wearing a size 13 means that packing just two pairs of shoes uses half a suitcase. Up to and including this trip, he chose his jumbo-sized suitcase (but not anymore!) to accommodate his XL stuff. His hands were full with his two bags, one huge and one carry-on. For me, I settled on a medium-sized suitcase, a computer roll-on bag for my presentation materials, and a handbag. That's more than plenty for me, a 5 foot 1 inch weakling.

Schlepping all our luggage, we looked prepared for a month's stay in Singapore.

More than 22 million passengers flew through BWI (Baltimore-Washington International) last year, and of course many of them were repeat fliers—including me. When I was a child, my family visited Friendship Airport (as it was called then) and watched planes take off and depart. Built in 1950, the airport was a fascinating destination for Marylanders. When I look at old photos of passengers, I see ladies in hats and gloves and gentlemen in suit-and-tie. You dressed up for flights.

Fifty years later the magic of flying would never be the same again, and passengers learned what TSA stood for. (The annual budget for TSA this year is more than $8 billion.) Like many others, I spend hours and hours stranded in airports and occasional train stations—occupied by gazing at magazine racks, buying gum, and fiddling with phone apps.

A writer in the Washington Post Travel section recently asked the question, "How desperate are we for a better flying experience?" (Oh yeah . . . we're definitely desperate!) Security checks are bad enough, but when they took away providing food in coach, things got ugly. "We're tired of eating Cinnabon for dinner,"said a writer for the Washington Post recently," napping in torture chairs and sitting on the crumb-littered floor to charge our gadgets."

Forward thinkers after 9-11 started to figure out that passengers spending lots more time in airports would spend lots more money while they were waiting, but the recession slowed down lots of airport upgrades. Now, though, it appears that things are picking up for beleaguered travelers. Airports are looking more like malls, with all sorts of diversions and pleasures coming our way. In 2020, I hope we'll look back and laugh (gallows humor!) at the awful travails we travelers put up with.

One thing the struggle has done for travelers is to make us more savvy. George Clooney's character in the 2009 movie Up in the Air became my travel guru. He made his living out of a suitcase flying all over the country firing people—not the part of him I connected to—and made an art form out of negotiating airports with panache. I found myself scrutinizing which security line to choose based on his lessons to a subordinate flying with him in the movie. I began to fell smug about the speed and efficiency of my every move in airports and train stations.

Ah, yes, there is a certain pride that goeth before a fall.

On our trip from San Francisco down to Menlo Park, we used the BART (Bay Area Rapid Transit), which our friend in Fresno (our last destination) assured us would be easy and convenient. He assumed, rightly so, that with all our collective travel experience, this would be no problem.

Automated ticket machines on train and subway walls should be psychiatric tools for determining stability/instability levels for patients. You face them with trepidation, certain from the outset that they will induce frustration and eventual anger. Since Matt has considerable subway mileage in New York under his belt, I hung back from the machines deliberately, deferring to his masculine instincts, to avoid the struggle. Patiently (and without any profanity) he managed to purchase two one-way tickets to the proper destination with his credit card. Gallantly, he handed me my ticket and proceeded through one of the turnstiles. (We hadn't noticed, unfortunately, that there was a wider turnstile lane designated for travelers with luggage.) As I approached a turnstile, I shifted my luggage with annoyance, already quite perturbed that my work stuff would plague me for the remainder of the pleasure part of our trip. For some reason (which always sounds so dumb in the re-telling), I carried my BART ticket in my left hand, unusual for a right-hander. Into the slot it went. I waited for the turnstile bar to swing down, releasing me to the other side where Matt stood watching. After an interval obviously too long, I heard the mechanism of the turnstile to my left swinging back down into the closed position. I had, of course, put my ticket into the wrong slot.

Although Matt stoically avoids cursing when annoyed, I do not. I railed at the turnstile, furious at my own stupidity but taking it out on the entire transit system. The ticket, which had cost more than $10, would have to be replaced . . . or not! I think I uttered something like, "I'll be damned!" as I shoved my luggage piece by piece under the bar and then ducked under it myself. A passenger behind me, apparently more amused by my antics than annoyed by the assumption that I hadn't paid, called out, "Woe, Shorty!" with a smile in his voice.

We re-grouped on the other side, both of us pretty sure that some unseen camera had caught the whole action and that we would be stopped immediately by someone uniformed. Nothing happened. Off we went, flustered but slightly amused by this episode, which turned out to be a mere prelude to what lay ahead.

A long escalator led down to the tracks. Already wary, perhaps, of my volatility under pressure, Matt insisted on relieving me of the larger of my two suitcases, exchanging a smaller bag of his for my burden. This time I preceded him as I rolled onto the moving staircase. At the bottom, I rolled off easily and turned to watch Matt behind me. To my dismay, I realized that he had positioned one large suitcase on the step in front of him and pulled the other large one behind him. As he descended toward me, time slipped into slow motion as I anticipated and then witnessed what was to come.

As the first suitcase hit the bottom, it lodged against the horizontal plate where the accordion steps meet the solid floor. All six-feet-one of Matt careened backward onto the suitcase behind him, which in turn fell backward onto the passenger behind him, and the domino effect continued up the crowded stairway. I was sure in that instant we would spend the night in one of two places: a hospital or a jail. I leaped forward and dragged the offending front suitcase off to the side as a man grabbed Matt's arm and yanked him forward. The passenger immediately behind him, a small Asian woman, popped up as if out of a jack-in-the-box, declaring, "I'm okay! I'm okay!" I have no recollection of any other sound. It all seemed to take place in a vacuum of time and sound. Even now, as I play it back in my mind months later, it takes on the surreal quality of an altered movie clip. Matt, however, recalls one escalator passenger hissing at him as she passed, "They do have elevators here, you know."

The enormity of the danger froze us afterward. Like countless others who experience the moment after an accident, we tried just to breathe for many minutes. Fear cut off any possibility of speaking to one another beyond probably a series of, "Oh, my god, Oh my god, Oh my god . . ." Like before at the turnstile, we waited for someone to arrive and arrest us. Again nobody came. Eventually we collected ourselves, physically and emotionally, enough to move away from the spot near the base of the escalator where we had stood, stunned.

On the train platform, we sat shakily, still too rattled to speak of it. Finally, torrents of 'what ifs' flooded out of us. Gratitude engulfed us.

I'm ashamed to record the last effect of our colossal clumsiness. After the relief and gratitude had time to settle in, we collapsed into fits of hilarious laughing—set off by one of those sideways glances between two guilty parties. Released by wave after wave of bent over belly laughter, we spent the ride retelling and retelling every second.

"The only aspect of our travels that is interesting
to others is disaster."

Martha Gellman

Unidentified escalator, Anywhere USA

"If you're going to be able to look back on something and laugh about it, you might as well laugh about it now."

Marie Osmond, singer

Bottoms Up!

"The chief reason for drinking is the desire to behave in a certain way, and to be able to blame it on alcohol."

Mignon McLaughlin, journalist

I left you dangling about that other 'notable alcoholic memory' didn't I? This one involves a silver Porsche. How could you not read on?

In 1978 it was apparent that my first marriage was in tatters (as they say). Escape beckoned. Convincing my husband that separate vacations would be practical, I headed off to visit friends in Frankfurt, Lucerne, and Paris with our ten-year-old Karen. Upon our return, he and our twelve-year-old Jeff would venture out to the West, especially the Grand Canyon. No problem with dog care and house watching, right? I must have been convincing.

Karen and I flew to Frankfurt on August 7, 1978 where we were met by Hans, a German teacher who had stayed with us in Ellicott City as part of a teacher visitation program. Having been to Germany during the 1976 bicentennial, I savored repeating experiences with my daughter and adding some new ones.

It was in Lucerne, Switzerland, though, that the magic came to us. Coincidence makes for great stories. Founded in 1178, Lucerne, resplendent with the celebration of the city's 800th birthday, greeted us with its surprise. Why our friends Markus and Walter hadn't prepared me for this wonder I can't imagine. Heraldic banners festooned the streets, musicals and dramatizations entertained. And smack dab in the middle of our planned stay there, a special performance and banquet took place. As the visiting American, I was awarded a premium seat next to the financier of the celebration.

(Karen spent the evening at home with Markus' relatives. If she, too, had been invited, the evening would not have taken the turn it did.)

Champagne flowed. (I told you this would be a story about alcohol.) I thought I was more inebriated by the setting than the alcohol, but I think that was a tie. The Swiss financier, also named Walter, bedazzled me with elegance and charm. I made no secret about my marriage and he made no secret about not caring. (Does this sound like a Nora Roberts romance? I swear every word is true!)

I'm sure I was novel and glib. Americans always seem novel to the reserved Swiss, and when I'm alcohol-enhanced, I can become glibber than glib. I weighed 110 at the time and looked trendily U.S.A. Perhaps he thought I was well off, and I said nothing to dissuade him. Mentioning that I would travel on to Paris after Lucerne helped the impression. Markus and Walter regarded me with sidelong glances of amusement, the bringers of someone new to the table. They also said nothing to dispel the notion of a daring woman who gallivanted around Europe at will—swilling champagne, scattering banter, titillating hosts.

At 1 a.m., my beau for the night suggested a drive out to his villa. If it hadn't been for Markus' and Walter's consent, I wouldn't have left. (Leave me that shred of decency!) If Nora Roberts really were writing this, she'd invent exactly what happened: I was led to a posh underground garage below the nearby casino where he walked to his silver, leathery, splendid Porsche. Did I babble anything intelligible while he tucked my hem beside my legs and checked to see that I was properly settled in the embrace of a car that cost more than my house?

Surely the moon was full. Surely the road wound through Thomas Kincaid scenery.

(*The* Fifty Shades of Grey *trilogy has dominated the book market since its creation in 2011. I'm one of those readers who found the eroticism spoiled by the sophomoric writing style, and yet, the paragraph I'm about to write will sound straight out of E.L. James, the British novelist who created the antics of Christian Grey and Anastasia Steele. So hold your nose and keep going . . .)*

His villa, some thirty minutes away, perched upon an elevated bluff with stone-buttressed terraces stepping down to Lake Lucerne. Promising additional delights, the glow from the villa backdropped our stroll along the terraces. Leaving me momentarily to savor the lapping of the water against the stones, my host approached the villa to fetch a bottle of champagne, which would undoubtedly exceed in excellence what we had already drunk at the banquet.

(Here's where my story departs from a romance novel.)

A dog barked somewhere up toward the entrance to the villa. I turned toward the sound, thinking perhaps the owner's pet might not welcome me. Swiveling, I lost my footing, pitched forward off the edge of the terrace and plummeted some eight feet into the lake. The water was quite shallow, and so I hit the bottom with my bottom.

Why I was standing so close to the edge is stupid and explainable. I was tipsy. (Never has that word seemed so apropos.) Drenched and mortified, I sat for a moment to assess the damage. Falling boozily was probably less harmful because of my looseness; no bones seemed broken. My derriere hurt like hell, however, especially the left cheek, which had borne the brunt of my fall. Despite that, the hilarity of the situation overtook me. Laughter burst from me—first as regular ha-ha, then as unrestrained guffawing.

Mr. Wonderful appeared above me, alarmed of course. A lawsuit flashed in his well-heeled consciousness. Clamoring down, he lifted and examined my body for disaster. (I had imagined him exploring my body in a different context!) My primary thought was about my hair, an unattractive, dripping tangle of soggy hairspray.

He drove me back to my hotel (and no doubt had the interior of his Porsche cleaned the next morning). I never saw the interior of his villa. Gallantly, he repeated his concern throughout the drive until certain that I really was okay. I remember the ride only vaguely.

The next morning I stood in a hot shower for a very long time. Toweling off afterward, I glanced over my shoulder into the wall-length vanity mirror. A larger than a dinner plate-sized bruise covered the left side of my butt. I marveled at the angry blend of purple and red in the morning sunlight.

Later that morning a long white floral box was delivered to my hotel door. Inside was one perfect long stemmed rose tied with a gauzy bow and a note that read, "You are the craziest American I've ever met."

Finishing the trip in Paris was another story I'll keep for some other time.

Remorse? Never.

Karen in Paris 1978

"To err is human, but it feels divine."

Mae West

Last Thoughts

Richard Branson kissed me a couple of weeks ago. Although the encounter was a scant few seconds and was certainly forgettable for him, it gave me enough giggle to brag about for days.

He happened to have dinner at Clyde's restaurant in Columbia at the same time I was having an unexpected dinner on a delightful and lucky Friday night. After three glasses of wine and an embarrassing number of glances in his direction, I had to approach him. As he signed for his check and prepared to depart, I slipped up to his table. Responding to my hurried compliment, he leaned over and kissed me as a man would who's practiced in constant female attention.

I'd like to say that it's not about his money, and indeed, he's handsome enough to make an encounter memorable. But $4.2 billion. Come on. The Virgin empire builder?

I don't apologize for my blatant school-girl crush. The man has class in a big way, funding an array of causes that demonstrate his optimism for an improved planet. In 2000 he was granted knighthood for his services to entrepreneurship. (Oh, yeah . . . make that "I kissed *Sir* Richard Branson.") Last year he opened the world's first commercial spaceport for Virgin Galactic and plans to be in the forefront of space tourism. Next year we should see his first $200,000 apiece passengers launched into suborbital space. (Galactic currently reports 500 bookings.)

And then there's Felix Baumgartner, a daredevil Austrian who recently jumped from a platform 128,000 feet above the surface of Earth and broke the sound barrier with his body.

Branson and Baumgartner are important to me (and of course, to many others) because at a time when we feel particularly tethered to the problems of our little planet, these two prompt us to look outward and push toward solutions.

As 2012 winds down and a bitter election draws to a conclusion, I begin to anticipate what's around the corner. Each birthday jolts me with new urgency, and the next one won't be any different. I will never gracefully accept 'slowing down,' so I must look for inspiration to individuals who defy gravity (literally and figuratively).

After I watched Baumgartner's successful landing in New Mexico (along with 8 million other YouTube watchers) I was captivated by the story of Joe Kittinger, Baumgartner's hero and mentor, an 84-year-old retired Air Force Colonel whose voice we heard talking to Felix. Kittinger made a record freefall jump from an open gondola in 1960, fifty-two years ago. Baumgartner wasn't even born until 1969. The two men seemed merged during the jump—one young enough to perform physically and one old enough to advise him.

Anjana Ahuja, a British science journalist wrote a comment after the feat that struck me more than any other: "He [Felix] kept the dream of space as a playground alive." The connection between my Branson kiss and Felix's jump meshed together when I read what Branson's CEO of Virgin Galactic had to say about Felix's contribution to space exploration (and certainly to space tourism).

How often I hear that everything happens for a reason. I need people like Kittinger to remind me of the worth of wisdom and longevity, and I need others like Branson and Baumgartner to remind me what courage looks like. Perhaps it will seem like a stretch to others, but I have no problem believing that as I finish this book and look forward to the next, the kiss and the jump were a signal to move forward in my own humble ways.

German smoker, Old Traveling Lady